Red Wine
And the
Bles'sed
Monkey
By
Tyla

EbonyEnergy Publishing, Inc. (NFP)
A division of The GEM Group
Chicago, Illinois

Red Wine and the Bles'sed Monkey
Copyright©2004
Tyla

EbonyEnergy Publishing, Inc. (NFP)
A division of the GEM Group
Permissions Department
P.O. Box 43476
Chicago, IL 60643-0476

ISBN: 0-9722795-6-3

Library of Congress Control Number: 2004110855

Cover Design: Na'Tasha Smith, Big Pink Designs, Inc.
Technical & Audio Support: Rasaki Solebo & Steven D. Hayes
Edited by: Douglas Long

Printed in the United States
First Printing
EbonyEnergy Publishing, Inc. (NFP)
A division of The GEM Group
www.EbonyEnergyPublishing.com
P.0. Box 43476
Chicago, IL 60643-0476

Dedication

You are the brightest stars in my life...

Latoya
Lashae
Tristen
Breanna
Martin
Rebecca
Michael
Lady Kennedy

Acknowledgements

Hallelujah!

I praise the heavenly Father for the gifts that he continues to bestow on me and for the wonderful people he divinely places in my life and experiences. And Though I can never truly find all the right words to speak completely my love, admiration and gratitude to my loving mother, Delores Lloyd, I pray that all I do say conveys how very much you mean to me. As for my sisters Charlene, Nicoa and Jacqueline... Where would I be without you? I love you as you are in all of your greatness and fearlessness to weather the storms of life and laugh out loud at its adversities. You've taught me well and I'm humbled in your grace. You make me proud to be me. Thank you, thank you, thank you... To my dearest friend in the world, Cheryl Katherine Wash, You make all the difference in everything I do and Ron OJ Parson, may the adventures never stop and the memories last forever; Tawanda and Ronald Wright, for your unyielding love and support, Kelly Roberts, for listening when everyone sane was asleep. Dr. Karen Ellis, you inspired me to try harder; Vincent Cirrincione and the entire management crew for helping me with the legwork. And to all of my friends who have heard all of my poems when they were in their birth and merely incidents in my life. And it just wouldn't be right if I didn't pay homage to my ancestors, great and small, known and anonymous, that sacrificed for me so that I may write this book, that my voice may be heard, that my experienced be known and that my place in this world be planted in solid ground and founded on soil rich with history.

Wow! I am so blessed!
"I'm making it one flight at a time! One flight!"

Tyla

iv

A Special Thanks

I am most grateful to my friends at EbonyEnergy Publishing, Steve D. Hayes, Rasaki Solebo and Na'Tasha D. Smith for diligence, patience and love. You embraced me, weathered all of my artistic storms and diligently forged ahead on the uncertain path that is I. I will forever feel eternally blessed, amazed, overwhelmed and humbled by your efforts.

Table of Contents

"I don't write poetry...
Life happens and poetry is written."

Tyla

Introduction

Red Wine and the Bles'sed Monkey is a glorious walk through the inner most personal moments in my life. I have learned a great deal from every person I've ever met even as the lesson to be learned traveled on the heels of an exit or at the foot of despair. I've tried to take those moments and the lesson they taught me and create a stronger, better me. Many of the pieces in *Red Wine and the Bles'sed Monkey* were actual journal entries that read with the flow of running water into the depths of me and I found a need to share them with the world.

As an actress, I have lived a great deal of my professional life on the stage, living the creations of other extremely talented playwrights. It was a welcomed journey when first I stood before an audience and shared a little piece of myself. It was then that I truly realized the power and beauty of the spoken-word. I realized how much healing could erupt from the poems I had written. I saw a light shine not only within myself but also within others, as I spoke not only from my heart but also to theirs. I've performed before many, of all races, creeds and colors, individual from all walks of life, firmly seated on all sides of politics and religion and what they have taken from my poetry has open even my eyes to new thoughts. I welcome all people to share in little *Red Wine...and* maybe together, we can get those *Bles'sed Monkeys* off of our backs; because where you stand may be where someone else wants to sit and where you sit may be where someone only needs to rest for a while. All I ask is that we try to understand the next man's journey.

Growing up in Chicago the youngest of four siblings with an absentee father and on the bare minimum life had to offer shaped me without me realizing that some of the shapes were merely impressions others had of me and that I adopted for lack of anything more positive to cling too. It has been a long walk into self-discovery. Where there is still a great deal to discover, I have answered a number of puzzling questions. My journey from this point forward is nurturing how much I can love openly, honestly and completely everyone I meet.

This intense collection of poetry, prose and song brought a sense of closure to issues I have carried around on my back, weighting down my spirit for years. I've managed to release some of them and grow up a little bit. As quickly as I released the pain that kept me suffering, I could see the seasons change. Now, I look forward to every new leaf on the tree of life.

Falling Out Of A Tree Can Hurt...
So Does Falling In Love!

When love finds our hearts it creates an energy within us that is so indescribable that even the most obvious of the obvious falls into the corners of our minds that are oblivious to anything and everything that doesn't feed the joy that is "you" in love. A thousand and one songs have been written recounting how silly love makes us, and how equally careless we become—all in the name of "love".

When we were kids we climbed trees, risked everything and we ran everywhere. Life was good and we were fearless, blinded by our glee. When we fell down it hurt and we cried. We did an amazingly simple thing and admitted that it hurt. We didn't care who saw or who knew, only that we were in pain and it was to be dealt with immediately. It hurt, all of it. From the bruise it left behind, the embarrassment of the fall, the entire experience - hurt. Even more amazing, was the freedom we possessed to show how much it pained us. Tears, sobs and snot flowed from us like running water. When it was over and the pain subsided, we'd get up and do it all again. Why not? After the shock of it all we had to admit "That wasn't so bad." In actuality, everything leading up to the horrible fall felt GREAT! Well, love is no different. The point I hope to make by saying any of this is that we should not become adults and hide behind the trees of your true feelings. Cry! Scream! Swear! Have a pity party if necessary! Then get up and do it all again. Life is for the living and feeling, Anything less is for the dead and lonely.

It may seem unlikely that the poems to follow are love poems. For they will not sing of blue skies and sweet flowers or of gentle touches, lingering gazes, proposals or marriage. On the contrary, they drag through the moments where love meets its end, its shadow, its victim, its villain, and its crossroad.

Love and hate are equal passions where they begin, meet or end, are usually ambiguous. When we hate, it is because we've loved and probably still do, but hurt makes us disguise the emotion with that seemingly, protective, armor known as anger. Recognizing the pain and letting it wash over your soul until it works its way out of your system is the only healthy solution. I'm not suggesting one should live in misery or wallow in self-pity but remember as life is for the living, love is for the feeling.

For years, the seemingly unrequited love of my Father, made me state openly and honestly to any who cared to ask, "I hate him." Finally, after 15 years I admitted, if only to myself, "I love him. I love him so much it hurts and I wish he loved me the same. I wish he realized how wonderful that job of being my daddy could have been and how much it truly meant. I wish he thought that being my dad was the greatest thing he could ever be in the world." It was the most honest moment in my life. I grew up and weightless at that moment. I did something I'd never thought to do before. I gave myself permission to be hurt, disappointed and in love. I stopped being a victim of my own anger and slowly I begin to find ways to forgive my dad.

Let love run wild until it runs out. Fight for it until it bleeds, cry until your tear ducts dry up and your heart scabs over, then open your soul up to love all over again. It's the only way to live.

With The End In Mind

I'll love you with the end in mind
Careful not to hold you too tight
Or say too much
For I know the end is near
Still though you are dear to me
It's clear for me
Without you
I'd sullenly exist
My happiness crashed against rocks
Chilled and petrified
No more sun to warm my blood
Nor seep nourishment into the marrow of my bones
Nothing walking me through life
See, I love you knowing that you don't love me
That you can't love me
That loving me would hinder you
Make you something
That you're not
A kept thing, a loved
Precious-jewel thing
A captured wild thing
Dying while I loved you, love you
So, I'll love you with the end in mind
Nearer though then I prefer it to be
Haunting my dreams
Catching screams in my throat
That chokes me till I wake
And see that you're still there
And that the end is still not here
Why my angel is sleeping beside me
How can my happiness exist?
Neighbored to my demise
Nursed by my desire
Exposed in your eyes

I watch you sleep
Wishing I could be that dream
That makes you moan and twist and smile
Can I dance under your eyelids, for a while?
I'll be a gentle invader
Speaking only when spoken to
Holding you close without smothering you
Warming whatever part of you
grows cold or afraid
And I'll remember to remember
that the bliss
Is only a dream
Night for you
Day to me
Your eyes closed
Your mind at peace
My eyes wide shut
My heart split open
My dream alive…
and living… with the end in mind
The End…
ticking away to Big Ben's
quarter, half, hour
365 Days, will I make it?
Is this a leap year?
Will this be it for me?
I want to touch you all the time
So that my finger tips remember you
when the end is here.
And I dare sometimes
that I'll share with you my fear
But I don't...
And I won't...
Because I know what that would do to you
And it is my responsibility
To keep my sensibility in check
And I'm trying but I admit that I am a wreck

Trying to love you with the end in mind
Though you are here with me, so dear to me
And still with me
But never hearing me
Scream. Silently
I love you...a lot...
But, I do it with the end in mind
Is that okay…
For today, anyway?
That I love you
I love you
With the end in mind

Dearest...

Dearest,
I love the way the day
Shows up in your eye each morning
And the scents of the world live,
In every strand of your hair

I taste the love of life on the tips of your lips
And I feel the beauty of the essences of living
In one seizing touch from you
And I know that I am alive
I adore you

You complete me.
For you are, the extraordinary life
Between every line, that describes me
And I love you

Your pulse completes the beat of my heart
Without you, I gasp for air
I know not one moment when thoughts of you
Fail to caress my mind's eye
And distract me
From the simplest of tasks

This is not an ordinary love affair
And I dare not believe it will ever end
For in its ending
I see only
A descending
Abysmal
Despair…
Never leave me
I love you

Piano Man

Remember me under your fingertips
My scent in your nose
See me when your eyes are open
And even when they're closed
Hear my laugh echo through you
When I'm no where to be found
Remember every whisper spoken
In every earthly sound

Taste my kiss on your lips
And in every bite you eat
Let the food that nourishes you
Taste a bit like me

And when it's time
To meet again
It won't seem so long
For your memory has kept me with you
Every hour I was gone

The Man I Mean To Love

The man I mean to love…
Will know what loving a woman means
He won't only want to love me
The way he wants to love me
And not at all the way I need to be loved
He'll see me in his life as he feels his heart beat in his chest
He'll wake in the morning and greet his first heartbeat with
A smile

He'll praise his divine creator
For his healthy, whole heartbeat
Then sit with it, and listen to it
for as long as a while can last

He'll never grow bored nor desire a change
The man I mean to love will love me equally
He won't expect anything less then his greatest expectation
And I will be that

The man I mean to love
Will live to love me back

The Analogy Of An Affair

This situation is completely motivated through Desperation
After extreme years of frustration...
And has little to do with anything...
Except temporary satisfaction...
Of irrational desires...
Set at the foot of confusion...
That is an affair
It has nothing to do with love
Or the future of love relations

A Tall Cool Glass Of My Soul

I poured my soul out to you
And you handed it back to me
Bruised, battered and broken
A hopeless casualty
I cannot erase the whispers
That seduce my inner most ear
And sound like you
Why you have kidnapped
The moon from my earth
And night shall never be the same

April 21st

This is the day that he raped...
The normality of my life
And left me relentlessly existing
In this never-ending state...
Of d*eja vu*

My Deception N 2 Parts

Part I
On the outside, I wear a smile
While on the inside, I frown
Deep, deep and deeper
The me, that *is* me lay dormant
Deeper even are the words
That describes my true identity
I am not as I seem
One in mind
Confident in self
In touch with one's soul
Aware of the divine spirits
Proud of my blackness
In love with my woman-ness
Happy in life
Lucky in love
Reaching, touching, seeing, feeling
My goals

I know better the road of deception
For I have traveled it long enough
I have trudged its twisting, tolling roads
Climbed its steep, unyielding heels
And looked in my mirror at its creation
I have committed the worst deception
Of any thief, liar, cheat or chameleon
And for it, dearly have I paid
I have tricked my eyesight
So that I saw only that which was not there
I cheated my heart
And sold it short
Because of fear

I altered the normality of my coat
So that I may fit in
I spoke words of an adornment
That had no depth
Stole someone's heart
Whom I did not love
Then questioned why they wept
Lost myself in all the mess
Settled down into a life
Of misery and stress

Now, I pay the cost of my deception
Smiling on the outside
While on the inside, I frown
Feeling foolish and lost
My world, my life
Spinning out of control like a clown
My deception
A real tragic misconception of it all

Part II
My Heart
I sold you short, and now
I don't know how to fix the wrong I've done
You were there always
Never doing more then waiting patiently
But, I had fear
I had doubt
I had a need to be needed
And I gave in to that need
Even when the desire wasn't in you to be
Where I had placed you
I'm sorry

An ever so small voice spoke softly
Gently to me always
Telling me you weren't happy
That you knew of so much more that
Existed in the world for you
But I closed my ear
Placed a blanket over you
To warm the coldness that began to grow
And grow

Like a well planted, and well watered tree
Separation and Isolation grew
And grew
Time knew little of you
Before I had placed so much about you
That even I, now
have trouble recognizing when what you feel is real
Righting a wrong is my duty to you
Forgive me
Can you forgive me?
Can you excuse the abuse…
And trust me again?
I promise to right the wrong I've done to you
If you can just keep believing
Keep pumping
Keep loving
Keep trusting me
I know you're there
I feel you
Every time my blood flows from you
I feel you
My dear
Lonely
Sheltered
Forgotten
Abused
Heart

24

Maestro

This is a day
I'll always remember
A cold day
In the middle of December
When trees were undressed
And the sky white,
Summer's gentle sweetness
Was far away
And winter had bedded down
For a few months stay
The wind chill factor
Was a driving force
And my love life was topside
On a life size course
My heart was shaken
Bruised and broken
And my banged up head
Could barely recall
The last words spoken
Said my love to me
In the odd hour of night
"It's over between us. You know I'm right."
An orchestra played behind his words
The string section was my tears
As they strummed down my face
My clumsy breath muffled the horn
And stifled its grace
And my knees drummed and knocked together
My heart struggles to burst from my chest
And follow his feet on to the street
The cymbal crashed behind the car door
And the Alto's screamed as he drove away
The Baritones carried me back inside
And I fell asleep wishing my Maestro died

Simply Blue

Like lightening, you set my soul on fire
Burned me with your passion
Raped me with desire
Feverishly snatched and tore at my core
Wrestled my naked heart
To a dirty cold floor
Then left it there amongst all
The love and lost weekends
Forgotten and sore
To survive or die
Simply blue is me
When I think
See
Worse, even
Need
You
I watch a phone that doesn't ring
Smother my tears with a pillow
Hope you can hear my heart scream
Wrap my arms around by body tight
Stare at your picture
Till I fall asleep each night
Counting backwards
To the day
You
Last
Called
Me

Once

I wanted him to want me
Dream of me as I did of him
But it was not to be
He had his life and I mine
And never shall the two again meet
But I dreamed of him wanting me
Every time I wanted him
And until my dream comes true
My dream will have to do

Shaken

I thought of you and smiled
I wanted you and couldn't have you
I love you because I do
And nothing explains it
Any better then that
I thought I might wait for you to love me back
But that might take to long.
You've got other things on your mind
So I'll let you love the way you do
Or not love at all
Count our moments together as a coincidental fluke
A time when life, love and pleasure
Sat at the seashore
And held each other for awhile
A threesome, a conundrum
What went wrong?
My waters are still shaken by the stone
And the wind cries your name
Every summer night
Or whenever I'm alone

Where To?

Do I live this lie?
Or leave this world behind
Start over some place new
Carry only my purse
And that which I do
Head to a land where
I'm not known
And make my way
Right?
I loved you as long as I could
Now that love is gone
Saw it catch the "A" train
Abandon my heart days ago
Leave it drained and empty
Now, all I love is what we had
And I need you to let go
Do I live this lie
Or leave this world behind
Start over some place new
Carry only my purse
And that which I do
Head to a land where I'm not known
And make my way right?

Nosey Pam

Maybe I'll just run away
Never have to look in another sad face
Leave this place
I've turned upside down
And find me a place
Where I'm not so down
But where will I run?
No, Where can I hide?
Where even the nosey will not pry
Where the world won't find me
And I can start over
Maybe get me a new name
To go with my new face
Disappear like a villain
Without leaving a trace
Remove my name from the mailbox
Drop my jewelry at the first pawnshop
Pass the places where my face is known
White out my presence from every moan
Who need this heavy shit anyway?
It only clouds the morning
And clutters the day
Leaving me still where I was
If I decide to stay
Yeah I think I'll leave this place
Wipe my presence from this life's face

Unconditional Love

My father didn't love me unconditionally
Or else he wouldn't have left
Moved out of our house
And of us, my three siblings and I
Forgot about

'Till this day
Fifteen some odd years later
I've never gotten over him
In every man, I see him
And because of him
I can't love
No…
I won't love
Any man…
Unconditionally

My mother loved one man
Her entire life
That man, *The man,* My father
Left her alone with three daughters and a son
To live an unhappy life
Filled with misery
Consumed with strife

My brother
Who had no choice
Became a man too soon
And left behind our life
He took on a world he knew nothing of
Except, the naked coldness of his mothers love
He was to survive off wit
And strength
Letting ten years go by

Before he and I
And I and he
Would meet again
And try
though we failed
To be friends
But still...
Our mouths were there to feed
My sisters and I
A daily rigorous struggle
For which my father did not heed
We became women
While we were still girls
Parents to ourselves
Providing basic food and shelter
Each dollar earned
Already delinquent on its purpose
Perfecting the skill
Of robbing Peter to pay Paul
A dexterity we had to master
If we were to survive
At all

I don't remember my father leaving
Just that he was gone
The date and time
Of his final departure
Has no place in this turbulent song
Was it morning or noon?
He traveled mostly by dawn
And foolishly, child sweet
I always expected him to return
He always did in the beginning
First every three days
Then every other week
Then once a week on Thursday
And then...

I guess then, he was gone
He told me he was leaving
Silly child I thought it a lie
I watched him sign the welfare papers
When ADC caught my eye
"*What does that mean dearest daddy?*"
I inquired.
"*After **D**ad **C**uts out— baby girl,*" he replied
And then…I guess then…
He was gone

But, still I waited
With breath baited
While my sisters hated
And my mother wished
"*Daddy…Dearest daddy…*
Please make your ritualistic return"
But he didn't
And I was smitten
Until my mind
Told my heart
That sundown was not dawn
Left was not right
And that daddy
Dearest daddy
Would not
Has not
And will not
EVER…Return
I was devastated!
Of my home, he left me ashamed
Fleeting memories and his name
"*Have no friends over to visit*"
My elder sister explained
Else "*we be embarrassed*"
How could we explain
The orange electrical cord

Thrown over the back porch
And extending to the basement
Plugged in over the landlord's washer and dryer
Where we STOLE our life's basics

"Well…what did I need of friends?"
I learned to believe
Just another pair of eyes to stare
At the little food we had to share
Dare I show my true face?
To those that didn't care
"Because if my own father didn't
Why would they dare?"

My father left
Not my mother, but me
He forced me to learn…From others
What was his job to teach?

On the hills of his exit
Went much of me
"After Dad Cut Out"
With him went my trust
With his smile went my emotions
With his hands
Went my comfort with touch
With his departure from my life
Went the idea of love

Some days, most nights
I wonder if he knows
How much of me he stole
Or if he even cares
About the love we never shared
Does his mind ever run his big strong hands…
Through the pools of tears that I've cried?
Has he mourned that part of me

He left stranded to die?
I doubt that he knows
Or that I could ever tell him so
The severity in which he crushed
The heart ... of my soul
Because of him... *"Daddy's little girl"*
Has created a safe world
Where I cannot love anyone
Whose veins do not pulse
With the same blood as mine
I am selfish with my love
A precious Jewel...Never seen
Even I, am unacquainted with it
For it has been sheltered so long
I fear that it has lost its song

Thus...
Gifts make me no difference
And Love is but a word
Unconditional love...
Doesn't exist
Except, in a lonely mother's hug

This Thing Called Love

What is it that love…Real love…
True love…
Is suppose to feel like?

Should it feel like the wind beneath my feet
That guides me through every day
And nurses me through every night?

Should love
Real love…
True love…
Soothe like the ocean's waves
Calming me when I'm upset
Settling my soul
Taming my spirit
Erasing my fear
And rebuking my pain?

What about this thing called love?
The intangible, expandable
Demanding, enchanting, enveloping
Renewing, subduing, simple, silly
Smothering, chilling, amazing
Crazy thing called
Love?

When I feel weak over just the thought of you
Eating less because of you
Living? Drinking? Thinking? Dreaming?
Needing you?
Is that that thing called love?
Real love?
True, love?
How about when I talk

36

And all my thoughts include you
Can never elude you
Wraps around you
Makes me reveal tales of seducing you
Tying up friends' ears with moments spent with you
Now...
Would you call that love, real love, true love?

Hey what about when I see your face in every place I go?
In every man I know?
Hear your voice in every word spoke?
Smelling you, when it isn't you?
And not knowing how, this day
I managed to get through
Without ever seeing you
Hoping to just run into to you
So I can say to you, "Hey baby, I still love you."
Though we've been through, for a year
Plus, two!
Is that love?
Real love?
True love?

Am I in love?
Or am I insane
For letting go of the pain?
That you engrained
On my heart
When you refrained
From every saying
"Hey baby, I love you."
Back?!
Wait!

Do I love you?
Or just the idea of you
Because, now that I think about it
You were never true
And though this I knew
I guess, I hoped, somewhere
Deep inside of me
I could change you
So, of the two, that make the fool
Who?
Me?
Damn!
I don't get this thing called love

You're Going To Regret Not Loving Me

Why does loving you have to be so hard?
Why does the line between loving you
And hating you…
Have to be so thin?
Why do you have to love me so haphazardly?
When I love you from some place so deep inside of myself
I can't imagine ever not loving you
You're going to wake up one day
And you're going to regret not loving me
The way you *could've*
The way you *should've*
I'll be the one that got away
The one you meant to tell
"I love you and I don't want to be without you"
The one you meant to drop to your knee and say
"Will you marry me? Will you carry my name…
On your back and love me for the rest of your life?
Will you birth my kids and give them your eyes and…
My smile and your looks and my cleft chin?"

I'm going to be the one that when I walk pass you
you're going to think though you dare not say:
"How? How did I ever make that mistake?"
In every other woman, you will see ME!
In every, EVERY, person that walks by you, you will think,
ME!

You will kick yourself over and over again for letting the
Love that you had for me that you refused to share because
You didn't want to go that deep
You didn't want to feel that much
You didn't want to think that hard
You didn't want to go through that tumultuous love affair
To find me at the end of it!

You're going to regret not loving me
You're going to regret just one moment that made the
Difference in our life time
The one moment when I said
"I can't do this
I can't play at loving you less, anymore
I can't fake the funk
Or
Walk the walk
Without
Talking the talk
I can't have you beside me and all up inside me and not say
I love you or that I want to love you forever and always
Through my days and your days and all the tidal waves that
Will follow
I can't do this!"
And you said
"Well, then, we can't be."
That moment…
That…
"We-Can't-Be"
Will be something to torment you for the rest of your life
Because you couldn't let go of what you wanted or thought
You should be, to be what you needed to be with me
You're going to regret
THAT moment

You're going to smell me in the wind
Feel me next to you in that California King-size bed
And when your new girlfriend touches your foot or rubs
You in the way that I rubbed you, you're going to want to
Say to her "Don't…touch me like that!"
And she will not understand when you're her man
That it's not her, it's you, with me all over your flesh

You're going to regret not loving me
I'm going to be tied to you for the rest of your life
Tied to you loosely, haphazardly, in thought and dream
I'm going to be tied to you because you will never be able
To untie yourself from me
And the reason for that will be because you didn't want to
Love me the way you could have loved me when all I
Wanted was TO-LOVE-YOU and have YOU-LOVE-ME!

I'm tied to you rather you like it or not
Rather you want it or not
You've tied me too you for all eternity
I will be tied to you constantly,
And daily and hourly and secondly
I will walk through you so often that
The sky isn't going to look the same
No sunrise will ever feel the same
Because…
You're going to
REGRET
NOT loving me…
Watch!

And when that regret is so great and you can't stand
Standing alone or out of harmony with yourself
You're going to want to call me
You're going to think to call me
When your nights go by sleepless and your stomach unfed
And your work goes undone
You're going to need to call me
To see me, to hear my voice
Just
One
More
Time

And you're going to search yourself
Search your house
Search every shelf in your life hoping to find something
That I've left behind so that you can call and tell me it
Exists in your space and that you only want to return it, but
Your search will turn up nothing except your misplaced
love For me

And on Monday you'll say "I'll call her Tuesday."
When Tuesday has come and gone you'll say Wednesday
No, no maybe Thursday
Well, okay Friday for certain.
But the week will turn into months
And when you can't stand it any more
When you can't fight it anymore
You're going to sit down to call me

Overwhelmed, you'll hope you get the machine so that you
Can leave a message and not have to say all the things you
Forgot to say or planned to say or meant to say way back
When…
You'll pray with wicked intensity for that little box with my
Voice recorded onto it …
You'll dial my number, but hang up before it rings
You'll tell yourself *"This is crazy!"*
That you're being silly
That you're just calling to say hello
But your gut will know the truth
I'll know the truth
And you'll know the truth
Because more then anyone
I know every inflection of your voice and what it means
I KNOW YOU!
Seven numbers never frightened a man so much

But you'll dial
And you'll listen
Then you'll wait
And just when you're ready to give up
You get what you wanted and it'll feel like promise
"Hello. Sorry I'm unavailable to take your call but if you'll
Leave a brief message. I'll return your call as soon as
Possible. Thanks for calling and have a blessed day."
Beep!
Your sigh of relief will echo but silence will hold you

What should you say?
How can you tell me all that you have to tell me in this
30-second time warp of man verse machine
And just when you're about to hang up something you
Never planned happens
I'll surprise you
"Hello...Hello? Guess I missed it."
Just then, you'll swallow your pride
"Hello."
Your voice will be music to my entire being
I'll stand, chilled. I'll be frozen in love
Is this really who I think it is or are my ears playing tricks
On me?
"How are you?"
You'll say
"How am I? Loveless, lifeless, hopeless, desperate, lonely
But that'll come forth from my throat void of my heart as
Fine. I'm fine. And you?"
Sick. Can't sleep. Don't want to eat. Can't think. Nervous
But, that will translate from your quivering voice as:
"I...I really regret not loving you."

Your mask, for once, will fall away
And you will know that that's all I needed or wanted in my
Entire life
That everything else has been a mistake, a repercussion to
All the lost time
And it will be too late
Too late because now I'm married with another mans baby
And I never wanted to be but I am. I'm the one that
Got away - unwillingly

You're going to regret not loving me!
You're going to regret not loving me!

TODAY!

Scabbing Over

I'm going to dig you up out of me
Wash you away with alcohol
And glaze you over with acid
Leave the wound you left behind open
And pray it scabs over
Over your lies and the tears I've cried
Over your *cheatin'* ways
Just over
And after time has passed
You'll fall away
No sign of you will bruise me
Or leave even the most minute scar
You will have never existed
Like a bad dream
Forgotten before it's remembered

Numero Uno X

I am
I am
I am the test
From which he learned
To be his best
I am my dear,
His first wife
But now
I am
I am
His X
Hallelujah!

Shipwrecked (a self-portrait)

Ship wrecked
Lost at sea
That's the way I see it
That's the way I be

Why?

You called
Why?
I ride high for a while
Then I cry all night
Cause you called
Why?

Fever

Here it comes
Flowing all over again
And I'm just fighting back the backlash
Of dealing with you at all
Heard your message and stood still in my tracks…
Waiting for the reaction to take action
There it goes
A racing heart
A cold sweat
Flickering eyes
And a humming in my ears
More near and dear you are to me then the breath I breathe
Why do I let you womanize me?

Love's Tangibility

She always wanted love to be a tangible thing
That she could capture between her fingers
And stuff it into the pockets of her tightest jeans
Then wear them indefinitely
Imagine her surprise at the intangible
Untouchable thing called love

Rivers

Rivers were created
By a sad, sad woman's tears
She was afraid of being alone
Wearied of being wronged
Forsaken in her soul
Hopeless of it all
So she cried herself a river
Then threw herself in

Lonely

Lonely eyes see only the dark
Even when the sun shines bright
Lonely ears hear dreadful silence
Even when a twenty-piece band
Is in full swing
An empty heart
Feels emptier even more
When the one mortal it loved
Has left a scabbing sore

Immune

You've forgotten all that I remember
A shallow grave held me inside of you
Wind and dust and your fancy has undone my place
In time and space
Who I am or was to you
Is forgotten

Whew!

Thought I'd open myself up to love
Was ran over with misery
A tractor truck, six feet tall, a big baldhead
And a smile that fought with sun light
Ran me down with a smile on his face
Drag raced through my emotions
Then tossed them away
Worked me over till he wore himself out
Then bull dozed over to the next fool's house

Thought I'd open myself up to love
I'll never do it no more
I'm going to stick with companionship
I'm going to take it slow
Sip by sip
Watch everyone else get run over
Cause I've been there, baby
And I've done that

Give

Give a little piece of yourself
In every thing you do
Hold back the blood and tears
Just give pieces upon pieces
Of yourself away
Until your spirit is a kaleidoscope
For everyone else to enjoy
A shattered reflection of a person you once knew
Always giving just a little to much
Of a little piece of you

Living

I have heard my thoughts
In others' sorrow
And felt my joy
On the wings of tomorrow
I've been seduced with love
And overtaken by pain
Filled with grief
And driven nearly insane
Still I know
From deep within that place
That I often go
Today I feel
What tomorrow I'll see
And dare to understand
Living between
My Heart…making me the fool
My Mind…telling me what's right
My Body…weak and vacillating and
My Spirit…my life preserver

Gotta

Gotta' dream
Gotta' dream
Ain't no point in livin'
If I *cain't* keep dreamin'
Gotta' dream
Gotta' dream

Wanna B

Straight hair wears better
Black looks lighter on white
Beauty can't be that deep
If it's that dark

Healing

AAAAAAAAAAHHHHHHHHHHHHHHHHHHHHHHHH!

That hurt me daddy
When you dumped me like that, it hurt like hell
So I'm just going to yell until I feel better
Sometimes screaming is the only form of healing

AAAaaaaaaaaaaaaaaaaaaaaaaaaaaaaaaaaahhhhhhhhhhhhhhhh!

Using Somebody

Use my salt?
Breath my Cooking?
And dirty my sheets…
But—you don't need me?

Routine

Crap
Traps
Mishaps
Saps
Long naps
Then do it again

Season

Am I in season again?
Haven't heard from you
Since God knows when
Guess my name is up
Time for another spin
Of the roulette wheel
Now you've called
And placed your bet
Well, I'll pass

Clockwise

Somebody hurt me
Now, I done hurt somebody
Suppose somebody gone hurt
Who ever is next?

Won't be no stopp'n the pain
Until it makes its way
Back…
To me again

Whose Fault Is It Anyway?

Oh no! Things aren't going so well! Every day is harder then the next. Suddenly the glass isn't half-full it's half-empty. And you just realize that every day you live...you die. Why weren't we all born with a silver spoon in our mouths? Why didn't our so-called "Parents" invest in Nike, Microsoft, or Subway? Hell, even Wal-Mart! Who, what, when, where and how, did we end up here? Well...that's simple. Believe it or not, heed it or not, you...we, choose to be.

When I've been fired from a job, laid off or just quit, proclaiming, "I'm nobody's slave!" I never blinked and eye. I'd say, "So what! It's not what I want anyway." And within a week, I would have found a new job. It was really that simple, that uncomplicated and that divine. I had that much faith in myself and it showed. Why? Because my perception became the reality. My greatness was so beyond what I was doing at any office, behind any desk, answering any phone and punching any time clock. It was ridiculous to care even a little. The greatness I was destine to achieve was evident to me, if no one else, and I walked around with my destiny and my faith and my indifference, like a gigantic staff. In my world, only my destiny was important. Everyone else was in place to assist me, advance my knowledge of the world, to be pawns in my play. I was destine to live my life my way, by my rules and when I had indulged myself enough, I would moved on, forward and upward determined to manifest my destiny. But...

But...But what, you ask? With that powerful paragraph, there exists a "but"? Yes. But...there was still an issue, which stifled me for years. I contemplated its existence constantly. Why, was it then, that with such an impressive level of faith and confidence was I unable to manifest the same reality in my true dreams and desires? Why was my climb to artistic success such a foreboding struggle?

Well...believe it or not, heed it or not... that too was simple. My perception within this particular area was loaded down with all of the fear I'd learned over the years. I couldn't believe it. Had someone asked me about fear I would have denied it's presence in my life. But, I would have been lying. I had fear and doubt and shame. These are some of the strongest forces in life, sure to hold you down and back. I had swallowed the doubt and fear of others and let it fuel my own shallow faith. I began to blame them for everything. "Had they not spoke so much doubt, if they would just give me a chance, if I was this or that..." In truth, I lacked the faith I needed to move the mountains in my path. I had relinquished my power to call into existence only those things, which I desired, even as I called into existence those things, which I didn't want and strongly disliked.

One day, during a rather lengthy pity party, I looked in the mirror and saw only me standing there. It was a gargoyle that looked like me. I saw a weakling, hanging around in my space and clouding my reflection. I asked myself, the Gargoyle, over and over "What is it that I'm doing wrong? What am I missing? Why was everything so hard for me? How could I change it?" Wait! What did I say? The words resonated and hung in the air and I stood mesmerized as I looked at myself and began to like something about the person I saw. It was small...maybe the nose... No. Maybe it's the eyes. Definitely, that smile. It was as if I had been slapped in the face with the hand of my reflection and it felt good. "How can I change it? How can I change it? How can I change it?" It was then that I realized that I was the cause and affect. Everything not gleaming in my life lay at the will of my faith in myself. I was the culprit. It was then that I decided to be catalyst.

We have an unlimited supply of what we need within ourselves and we must challenge ourselves to demand nothing but our complete best. Naysayers exist and there purpose is great, for if it were not for them the world would be flat, man would never have made it to the moon and I most definitely would have never written this book.

If we are to be true optimist and one must be an optimist to have faith, then you must accept that the barer of bad news can also be the chariot of greatness. Everything depends on the perspective in which you see, hear and feel things.

Embrace life! It's your work of art. The world is your canvas, be creative and have fun.

Back Sliding N2 My Blues

There goes my blues again
I was wonderin' where it's been
It's wrapped up in that horn
Taking me back to the day, I was born
Yeah, listen to my blues
It's making me heavy; this paying dues
Like a cloud on a rainy day
I'm weighted down in a bad way
Murphy's Law… at work again
One foot up…is another one down
Yeah my blues is back
And it's totin' a familiar frown
See, there's my daddy's face
Staring at me in the mirror
But look there at my momma's eyes
Crying tears from mine
Now, whose smile is this I wonder
Always turned under?
Just where do these lines lead
that run off the edges of my face?
I wonder if just one runs
Into a happy place

Yeah, my blues is back
Think I'll take a drink
Shake this shit, man… it stinks
A shot of Jack Daniels
A couple of lines
Of a little white powder
Hell, in *no time*…
I'll find me something to be proud of

Maybe follow this here line
At the corner of this, here eye
Fine me some place to fly
Or cry
Or just die

Man, I'm getting old
Without ever feeling young
Strung out on depression
Stuck in a recession
Addicted to pain
Not sure who to blame
Loaded down with guilt
Chained to shame
Call it "*Stormy Monday*" or
"*Blues for Mr. Charlie*"
"*Blue Moon*" or "*Kind of Blue*"
I got it bad...
And don't know what to do

And don't nothin' sing about it
Except that music Miles plays
Or maybe Billie can tell you
How I feel
"*Good Morning Heartache*"
Billie, baby. That's real

You got blues for me Mama
Like I got blues for you
You got blues for this daughter
That's lost and don't know what to do
Blues from your Mississippi sky
Born by the river, Baby
Dying on the tracks...

Tracks of love
Tracks of life
Tracks of "Free Will"
Tracks of strife
Tracks that lead
From my Momma to me
Blues—
I got it
Worse even, "its" got me
See, if I had grip on "it"
Blues I mean
I'd sat that bitch free
Let her ruin somebody else's day—you know
Weigh down their happiness
Age their face
I just…I just wanna' SCREAM
"I got sun shine on a cloudy day"
Instead I just begging
Always beggin'
This…
"Ill wind blow away,
You're blowin' me no good"

You got blues for me Mama
Like I got blues for you
You got blues-
For your daughter
That's lost and don't know what to do
Can you help me Mama?
Nawwwww!
That's right, I forgot
You couldn't help you
F**k it then Mama
Here's to blues, baby
For me and you

Me And The Devil

Me and the devil done met and made a pact
Now he's my only friend
And I'm number infinite, infinity plus
Disgusted with the way things aren't just happening
They're happening just
Enough on the wrong side of things
To drive me crazy
Say I done sold my soul to the devil
And ain't no taken it back
But if things don't get better then they been
Me and my only friend
Gone have ourselves a spat

He says my soul is the ultimate cost
The sure win in the abyss
That I've lost against one x 2 damned many
Devil done had his hand in my pocket of plenty
And now he don't have to concern himself with steeling
And…I'm sold

Cause Me and the devil walking side by side
So You all better look out!
Cause it's as if I'm in love
And not that angelic, dynamic love
That hugs and rubs
All over and down and inside
Not that universal love
Grown from some comic oneness
Of man meeting women or…
Women meeting man
Where
A future of two's
An off springs…

Springboard...
Into a future of fake bliss
And routine lovemaking
Ahh! Hell No!

This love is dumbfounding
Spellbinding, bewitching and eerie
To the point of irrational thinking
And impossible dreaming
Of tangibles enveloping into each other
Where the impossible though volatile
Is expected
Where...NO!
Really does mean...HELL YES!
Lovers on a beach hand in hand
That's the Devil and me
I tried
I did
I tried to avoid his gaze
Evade his lust
fight off his lure
But being poor
Makes being hell bound
To profound
To believe
That day will ever come
And even if it does
How much of it will I really remember?

When I'm in cahoots
With Lucifer
What does eternal life mean...
When daily living...
Is twisted around the rent check
The car note, daycare, groceries, home phones
And cell phones
And that ain't even counting that one luxury

I sneak for myself
every now and again
Just to help me forget
That I ain't got SHIT
The bank values
Or call collateral
I'm living to die, baby
Working to be broke
Praying to maintain all of what ain't maintaining me
In any way I can smile about
And that's why

Now, somebody tell me
How can selling my soul be any more horrible
Then the road I'm walking...
Or the cross road
That never leads to any place 2 damned special?
Devil's foot ain't no bigger then mine
But he takes bigger steps into the future

Where ever I'm headed
He's gonna' get me there quicker
Then my
Moral, integrity riddled past and present
Code of honor
Has gotten me

See, the Devil looks just like he should
Big red eyes and long nails
Horns for ears and a tail
His fangs are teeth that tare at flesh
And crush SOULS
The Devil's got a bag of trick
And I done fail for every one
But he's also got a magic wand
That makes every WISH...
Come true

The devil's so "Damned" tough he can crawl into a bottle
Then, parch your damned throat
Seep from a pipe
And call your name
Transform into a fancy expensive material thing
That charms your third eye
That controls the hand
That knows where you keep your wallet
That owns the credit card...
With barley a limit
That you been saving
Just incase of an emergencies
And wouldn't you know it?
A "damned" emergency just sprung up

He can be the iris in that eye
That sees me as GREAT
Or create the plenty that flows from
Others pockets into mine
He can change the Romaine noodles
I ate last night
Into steak today

Devil can walk tall or shrink
Ever so small, smell good
Liquidate your emotions
And bankrupt
Your common sense
Whatever your pleasure be
Call on the Devil for help…
JUST ONCE!
And you'll be just-like-me

Cause—Me and the Devil walking side by side
And we got room for you

The Devil's my main man
My sure win, my soul mate
My homey at the gate, my better half…

And if Eve only convinced Adam to eat the damned apple
Then I'm going to serve up a feast of delectable delicacies
And finger feed them to the world
I want Eve to be remembered
As an after thought
To me
And ain't no turning around or running
So I'm just gonna' ride
I'm gone ride the devil like he's been riding me

And I'll see all you suckas real soon
Cause if you go on livin' in this
Monsoon of planes, trains and automobiles
That don't get you know where quicker
And asking Sir Hellalot the tyrant for time off to pee
You bound to give in
To one or two sins
And size don't count
Remember that, baby!
The penalty is the same-damned-amount
Hel?
Or Hades?
Can't neither one of them save me
Fighting for my soul
Cause in "their" pockets
I'm gold
But they don't grant wishes
And that's all this life is
So I'm gone sell my soul to the devil
And get a few wishes granted
While I'm still standing
And if what I'm saying is turning you off
Just give me a second…

And I'll turn you on-
Cause… I got it like that and…
{Me and the devil, walking side by side}
And we got room for you. Wanna' come?

*Greek Mythology

HEL: Hel is the daughter of Loki and the giant, Angurboda. She is the sister of Fenrir (Fenris-wolf) and Jormungand (Midgard Serpent). She is the goddess of the underworld. Her realm was Niflheim which was often referred to as Hel and her hall was called Elvidnir [Misery]. In her hall her table was called Hunger and her bed Disease. She was described as half white and half black.

HADES: Hades is the brother of Zeus. After the overthrow of their father, Cronus, he drew lots with Zeus and Poseidon, another brother, for shares of the world. He won the worst draw and was made lord of the underworld, ruling over the dead. He is a greedy god who is greatly concerned with increasing the number of his subjects. He is exceedingly disinclined to allow any of his subjects to leave his domain. He is also the god of wealth, due to the precious metals mined from the earth. He has a helmet that makes him invisible. He rarely leaves the underworld. He is unpitying and terrible, but not capricious. He is the king of the dead but death itself is another god.

***DEVIL:* The devil also known as Beelzebub and Lucifer, appears to be derived ultimately from the Sanskrit root div. In its strictly biblical sense the word is derived from translating the Hebraic 'Satan' into the **Greek** 'Diabolos', although **Satan** was not directly an evil or fiendish being so much as a tester of man's relationship to God. In this way the two distinct beings, Satan and Diabolos, were first confused and then later merged.

The Escape

Like a feather floating through the air
Pushed by nature's breath
Off a cool summers lake
I drifted...
Uninhibited by gravity

I bounced around in the clouds
Their cushions like a trampoline
I soared above the world
Too far for the human eye to see
I danced a crazy dance with the angels
To a drummer's wicked beat
And all that was bad, seemed good...
As long as I was asleep

Shoez

Where are the *shoez*
That covered my feet yesterday?
Somebody done moved my *shoez*
Now, my day all messed up

A Sign

I tried to look inside his soul
Beneath his berry black skin
Underneath the flesh that hides his gold
To reveal the treasures within
I looked into his beautiful brown eyes
That to me sparkled like diamonds
I caressed his full black lips with mine
And listened in complete silence
I held close to him
As he walked me through
His soul's lonely island
To begin his sullen tale
I watched him swallowed all that he had
"Your pride," he said, "It seems
Is all the black man has".
He cried his tears into my hands
And I wiped them away with kisses
I promised him love
Forever and always
He smiled and I thought I'd die
I watch the world lift from his shoulders
And glee dance in his smile
But, I got his letter Monday
Notification, of his suicide

Ya'll Trying 2 Make Me Hate Myself!

Dark skin blanketing me
Brown and glistening
Soft and sweet
Eyes that are brown too
Smiling from way down deep
Where all that exists makes me happy
I am a black woman
I was a black girl
I am an American
Born and raised
Proud and saved
But Y'all trying 2 make me hate myself

Hate myself because my hair ain't straight
Because my skin gets darker
Then it's already dark self, in the sun
Hate'n the melanin in my skin
Just cause you can!
Spitting insults at me with your nose turned up
Cause I carry my black self around
Like my people, make me proud
While Y'all trying 2 make me, hate myself

Pointing out all the bad U can find
Buried in my past
Wiping up all the ugly, you can predict
For my future
But I know what was
I know what is
I know what will be
And I'll scream it till the day I die
I'm black and I'm proud!
But Y'all trying 2 make me hate myself

Convincing the weaker reflections of me
That they want long hair that flows
Or that my brown eyes
Would look better blue
Using the world as your stage
Showing only reflections of you in my race
And calling them black
When their European rapist face
Is more prominent then their African mate

And that's okay cause they black that true
But so am I
Now you want me to accept..
That black is better then my black
Because my black is three shades darker
And my ancestral rapist is harder to find.
Because you've conceded to believe
That my momma's beauty
Blazing through me
Just ain't good enough for you
Y'all trying 2 make me hate myself.

Brothers! Oh, yeah I got brothers too
Out to do the same job to me as you
Cause you did your job on them
They bought the house, the lake, the boat, the Jet
And the bullshit 2!
Bought himself the right
To have a white girl
Abandon his black kids and split
On his black mother, sister, daughter, Wife!
Oh, he's trying to be down
And get down
With the capitalistic way
He's a…
Black clown, some of my black brothers
Because…

He believes I'm 2 much 2
Says I'm not nurturing, understanding, forgiving
Pleasing or pleasant
I've never seen a scheme designed so keen
Altogether
Ya'll folks make me wanna' scream
Why ya'll trying 2 make me hate myself?

Nurture, brother? I nurtured loving you're ass every day
When the White man puts out the statistics
That carries your future to the
Five, seven and nine o'clock news congregation
I say, "Bull shit!
My black brother will live
As long as I can reproduce another black brotha!"
Up lift another black brotha'
Educate another black brotha'

Understand! U demand
Every time my black mamma, took back my black daddy
Who had 2 leave 2 hustle 2 get ahead or so he said
Understand she did as she remade the bed he lied in
With one and two others…
And came home only with more of us
She understood, taught me to understand.
Why she closed the door and said
"Don't explain."
She taught me to understand the black man's plight
To "Forge and alliance to his fight, Daughter"
For in strengthening him you will strengthen us.
And you say I don't understand
Or that that white girl understand more so
No I understand you better then you think
Cause, your ideological break down is his-story baby
Not a miss-story

Forgive? I forgave every time you looked away from me
Made your millions and after set others like me, free
Changed your mind about who you were
And opened your soul up to B die-verse
Oh, I forgave
Hey, love *IS* color blind…
So, why you stop looking at me at all?
I guess your die-verse-city don't need me
You've got blond, and blue and red and green and yellow
So what do you need with another primary color like black?
You're the black piece of the puzzle blending and mixing
And fixing
But look in the mirror and what do U see?
Just another black man staring back at me
Asking me to forgive, again and again and again
Kobe Bryant, Michael Jordan, Clarence Thomas,
Tiger Woods…

Pleasant? How pleasant must I B?
Is it wrong to insist that you, my husband, my lover, my
Brotha'
Choose only me?
Pleasing?
What ain't pleasing about me exactly?
I guess I don't look like you would like me to look
Like you been brainwashed into thinking I ought a look
No blue eyes, no blond hair, no thin lips
No world in my corner telling me I'm a prize
Forbidden you from my fruit
You use to like your coffee black
Now you like it with cream too
And milk coats your stomach
Y'all trying 2 make me hate myself

Even got the Gay girls on your side
Talking about they don't like Sistah's attitude
And they can't get down with the way they groove
Heard one of them say… to the other, the other day
Sistah's got too much going on
And they carried it all around on their backbone
Say it's easier to get with a white girl
She's got a lot less drama
Going on in her world
Damn right she do!
That's what I been standing here trying to tell you
Y'all trying 2 make me hate myself

All hell, maybe I should just give it up
And get me a white girl too
Hope she can do for me what she does for all of you
Maybe make me to feel a little less black
And more accepted in the
Political, Successful, Powerful, Suburban circle

Show the world that I'm diverse
And open to change
This is what my love looks like.
Maybe adopt me a little brown baby
Show I'm willing to represent
The New "Millennium" family

I've been the backbone of this land
Nurturing, breading and feeding man
Now every bodies looking at me
Still not seeing that I am too
One of this Nations most prized commodities
Why y'all trying 2 make me hate myself?

But I've got to be strong and hang on
Because I'm black and proud of it!
And somebody's got to raise the
Little black child, till they all brown

Wonder if he going to grow up and hate me too
Cause monkey see, daddy…
Monkey do…

Born Free

Born free
Made wild and meek
Lost from the past
Looking blindly into the future
Totally missing the present
Born free
With your hands cuffed behind your back

Silence

How much it says when *it* speaks
Silence!
Between two lovers
Can mean passion beneath the covers
Or death of love
From one to other

Silence!
When it screams
Means so many things
The difference between extremes

Time
And Silence
Can answer defiance
And destroy the vowels
Of a husband's and wife's alliance

Silence!
Says it all
It's never heard
Until it's called
Hello. Goodbye,
Between two words
Belies silence
And indicator
That something which lived
Has now died
Silence!

More Silence

Silence happens!
My mind begins its wonder
Into the depths of my sanity
Teetering at the edge of my comfort
Pushing at my anxiety
Silence Please!
I need Silence!
A mist a room
Of faces and gloom
I see in the eyes
Of those who hide
Behind their lies
Silence!

But I can see
The lack and the need
Where ever there is silence
What should be said?
Becomes a fight
A need to conceive
A pregnant moment
Where silence
Does not haunt
Giving leave
Of the silence deed
Where whispers feed
In our minds ear
SILENCE PLEASE!
I need silence!

Survivor's Guilt

How can I discuss the loss that looms, when I cannot think
the thought or speak the words that tell the deepness of my
hearts hurt? My life has been raped, my soul shattered, my
spirit blown through with pain and fear marred with
survivor's guilt.

What does my life really mean if I'm not using it for joy,
For love, for infinite good?
Me, an invisible being in the face of all that makes all in the
World
What can I do?
Who can I help?
Who will I have touched when my fingers are decayed and
Unable to reach, to feel, to teach?

Today?
Today. This day, I love. I hate. Equal passions.
I hurt; I die with every being that perished on this brisk
September day
747, 911, 2001
The mark of the beast in human nature!
A tear, my tear is not enough to mourn the tears shed in that
Dreadful hour of goodbye.
We watch in disbelief, clinging to collective survivor's guilt
Thanking God, blaspheming God, questioning God.
What has man done?
If I had the answer, not one life would be worth its reason

I hate, I love, equal passions, devastation
So, I'll pray for forgiveness
I'll just sit here, at home, alone, alive and pray
And try to sort through the shock

We love you
To all those that didn't hear it this morning
I love you
Your death was so unnecessary, so wrong, so unexpected
Your stars shall light the sky forever
Forever!
Forever!
Forever!
As I live with Survivor's Guilt

Hocus Pocus

The magician stands before the crowd
And waves a wand about
He promises intrigue and delight
Trickery designed to deceive the naked eye
He is for me
America, the beautiful

Elusive Trickster

My heart is heavy, more so than any weight
Its pain runs deep, a dark abyss as turbulent as the sea

My life cannot catch up to my dreams and my dreams
Cannot catch the "Right" time, "time" being the skillful
Trickster that it is

Therefore, the Me that I dream to be is where I live and the
Me that is Me, for every one else to see, is an unfamiliar
Me, to Me, the dreamer

Why, I don't even know how to handle this *Me's* life
For it is the Me in the dream whose life and mind I am
Prepared to manage, whose ideas I know well

Maybe, I should just wake up and face reality. but then I'd
Just die, even as I lived. So I think I'll stay where I'm at

I opt to desire that the seeming appearance of things will
One day fail to seem so bleak, and instead give way to what
Lies beneath
For surely it will be the Me that I've always dreamed to be
Don't you agree?
Or, will the Me that I've always dreamed to be, always be
In a dream?

Piteous One

Love is the ultimate gift
Thus, we seem to hold on to it with all of our might
Keeping it from the anybodies
That never seems to mean the most
Or impress us enough
But, we opt instead to save our love
For someone special or something "special"
How sad it is when special never comes
And love is but a thought of what it could have been

My Mind

What things get trapped inside my mind?
That control and hold my thoughts like twine
I become stuck and subdued
Controlled and fooled
In a manic world of don'ts and do's
What has this society done to me?
That hated wretch from whence all is taught
Where my identity and happiness
And laughter is caught
I must now unlearn
What has been learned in order to discern
What is real, and what is true
An American—that will always be
African-American—First
My mind is shackled
Like our ancestral mothers
Hands and feet
When I free them
Then I shall know me

Sad Self

I am growing more and more depressed
I am starting to frighten myself
I have been so overtaken by the American dream
That eludes me at ever turn
I fear I would rather die
Then live miserably
I am afraid for me
For my woe is so heavy
That I rarely sit without a tear in my eye
I speak words that are plucked
From a plethora of lies
I've lost a handle on things
And am oh so tired of swallowing
The lumps in my throat
I see why she sits as she does
On the edge of the earth
Watching life in silver/gray and color
For it is merely a fantasy to be happy
And life to be sad

Fool

Once a friend walked up to me
And asked had I been crying
Foolish fool, who is a friend to me, has yet to see
That I am always crying or about to cry
That's all I do all day is cry
Foolish friend of mine

God's Irony

He drank to wash down
The bullshit he had to swallow
And hid his tears beneath his flesh

He froze his heart into a plate of steel
And smoked to burn out
The rot he feels

He cursed the sun
And praised the moon
Swearing his future
Brought nothing but gloom

The devil he believed was
Wicked and bad, but
Jesus he swore
Was a worse man

All the man wanted
Was to lay his body down
Forget his poverty
Escape his day mares
Block out his failures
Release his cares

He prayed for death
To bring him relief
But the man lived on
He and his grief

Gray Days

Seldom seeing the light in a gray day
Making my way to the top of a mountain
That's a fountain of failed dreams
Over rehearsed schemes
Of this time is my time
Or moreover
I got something nobody else has

I can feel my knees shaking, my faith wavering
And I'm crazy for even believing in that thought
That's bloomed behind my eyes
Some where deep in my mind
And got me reaching for a sphere
And pulling back an empty palm
With the lines in my hand
Forgetting to tell the story of my future

The Universe it seems has forgotten it promised me
A bag of gold in my youth
And I've yet to have any proof in the pudding
Me? Me? I'm nothing me
I'm just swimming in a fantasy of
Somebody's ecstasy
That has to catch up with me soon
Or I ain't going to make it

I've already dropped to my knees and proclaimed
"I can't take it. What's the score?
Where's the magic wand?
Who has the power?
Where do I sell out and sign up?"

I don't need mirrors
I don't have to look at my reflection
Hexing and vexing me.
I'm cried over and tired...
Tired of dreaming about being
On top of a world
That's only got room
For somebody
That ain't me

I'm counting the pieces of my broken spirit
And handing them over
Somebody help me or just saved me
From myself

Give Me A Minute

Looking at the world from a fetal position
Standing today on…
My own two legs don't seem possible
The world been showing me tough love
And I need a hug or just to get away
Dreaming of a better time, a glass of wine
And a smile on my face
Wind in my hair and something special to care about
But the in's and the outs have caused a drought all over my
Relationships
And my higher minds are dipping behind clouds
And keeping me low
I got to find the straps to my boots and hoist myself up
Do a couple more flips and turns to avoid the burns
And land on my feet
Search the hum of my soul to find that raging percussion of
My ancestral heart beat
I'm going to come out of this real soon
Wash away and down all the gloom
Stand on my knobby knees and be free
That's what I'm going to do
That's exactly what I'm going to do for me

Right now…
In this fettle hug
I'm just going to rest
Let all this heaviness ride me
But when the morning comes
I'll be prepared
Socks, shoes and blues
Ready for the run
Of a new day
I'll be ready

Sit

Sit
Sit
Sit
And wish, wish, wish
Or make it…
Happen

Hang'n On

Hey, Man
I'm listening to this music
Remembering when we were kids
And hang'n out was all we did
Nobody counting the pleasures or the pains

Taboo's In Culture

No one wants to admit the things they feel, especially when they are fueled by anger, or twisted around the pleasures and pains of sex. To cuss and fuss and cry and scream is unacceptable behavior, yet we all do it. The very thing that fueled what was once an eternal passion; has now turned its coat, and the mark of the beast seems bigger then life. I love...is now... I hate. What once felt good, now feels routine, and sometimes a little spice and vulgarity is just what the doctor ordered. It becomes just the thing that helps us over the hump.

Women have a role to play in society as do men. We are often so afraid to step outside of those roles for fear of what's to come and who may be watching. We overwhelm ourselves with question like: What if what I say isn't what others want to hear? What if what I desire isn't in fashion? What if...? What if...? What if...?

Stop crucifying yourself, others will gladly do it for you. Dare to be different. Dare to speak your mind. Dare to love openly and freely and most of all, dare to live your life, your way. Scream, moan, cry, shout, cuss and dare! Hell, double dare...then get over it. If it's acceptance you seek, try accepting yourself and being who you are.

Dirty Old Man

What is it about you?
That makes you think
I'm going to waste my youth on you?
If your dollar signs have blown your mind
And you figure every bottom has got a number
Then start the count with the amount
And keep your hello in the folds of your wallet

You figure I got no choice
Cause my need
Can be met
With your supply
That I can
Just
Close my eyes
And let you all up inside of me
There ain't no difference whose doing it...
If it ends with something that spends

So just lay your thoughts out
And spare the B/S about
Taking me out
Cause I don't like you
And this is about your money
And the fold between my thighs

And let me tell you
If age ain't nothing but a number
Then so is money
Start counting
And don't stop until
You pass your age by ten
Make sure it ends with three or four zero's
Cause then you can be my hero

And save the day.
My frankness making you frown
Then turn your elderly bones around
And ask my mother out

Living in the land of abundance and consumption
Has made a fool of you
65 and 25 ain't never about love
IF!
Grandpa or Grandma don't immediately follow

Using my ear to hear your fears would be just fine
If you could do the same to mine
But you want me to think
you only want to be my friend
And save me from the dogs of my day
Young men who can't and wont spend nothing on me
Won't treat me right
Or love me right
But ain't I got the right to decide that on my own?

Didn't you learn lessons the hard way?
And look at you...
with all of your loot...
You turned out and up okay
You want to use me old man
In ways, you'd never use your wife
And heaven forbid
If the things you think of
Your daughter did
Or somebody taught it to your
Granddaughter
You want me to be your young whore
While you live your lie
Idealizing your wife
Why she's the Bles'sed St. Madonna
In your life

Your head is on backwards
And your coat has turned
You're a sexual deviant
A predator with a pocket full of money
Sniffing up and buying honey
And using it to boost your ego
But in the end you're still
A little man...
Grown old
Praying to find
The fountain of youth
Between my young thighs
You can live the lie
Your money's bought you
Before you die
One more day hoping to
Capitalize off my missed boat
Or fallen hope
Elevated dream
And my lack luster spirit
You're trying to devour me
You dirty-old-man

What I Want

Want me with furiousness
That greets me at the door
Snatch away every stitch of my clothing
And rustle me to the floor
Caress my breast
With powerful hands
Then suck them down like lunch
Grab a fist full of my…
And whisper the things you want
Part my legs wide
And lick me till I'm weak
Make me say the things I've dreamed
But never thought I'd speak

Poochie

Poochie liked coochie
Shelby's coochie—to be exact
But, Shelby liked coochie too
Donna's—as a matter of fact
Donna was fond of Shelby
But took much more of an interest
In Bill

Girlfriend!!

He told me his favorite color was blue
And that of all of my dresses
The blue one was the best
Said he loved the way it hugged my hips
Caressed my voluptuous body
And made love to my eyes

Swore this here dress brings him to his knees
Mucks with his mind
And keeps him long after he's gone
Thinking of me
So I bought a slew of these
Ugly-Freakin'-Dresses!

When You See the Light, Fly Into It

That walk through the tunnel of despair is a valuable one. I challenge you. My new friends, I challenge you to face the looming shadows that keep you away from that radiating light at the end of every tunnel. For in the shadows lie the most profound lessons and thorough understandings of a better you, a greater good, and a solid sense of balance.

Red Wine and the Bles'sed Monkey is a collection of my thoughts and written manifestations of the first couple of decades of my slow drag through the "Tunnel to Greatness". I'm on the other side and let me tell you, I feel weightless. I'm standing in that radiating light armed and ready to go. I'm forging ahead into the next several decades.

Start rebuking the little monkeys, big monkeys or overgrown Apes that swing in the shadows, waiting to land on your back, and weight you down. It is then that you can sunbath in the weightless results that you will continuously create for yourself.

A Revelation

People, places, things in my life are changing
Reasons like season are revolutionize in there meaning
I'm seeing things that were before hidden
Feeling, feelings that before had me smitten
But now I don't scare so easy, I don't feel so needy
I question the source but not the notion
Knowing now that my emotions are the ocean
That provides me with the commotion to know better when
Something is wrong
That needs to be made right
Alone in my room or meditating my next move
I listen and I hear. I bare and I dare to be the child my
Creator wants me to be
I let go of the seeming appearance of things
And hold steadfast "to whom so every believeth without
Doubt that what he *sayeth* shall come to pass
Shall have it!"
See my Lord and Savior promised this, I read this
He told it to me through
Mathew, David and John the Baptist
I am, who I am and I am made divine
I'm moving out of my own way and letting my spirit shine
Why when I stand before a crowd
I silently pray
Don't let them see me God
Let them see you this day
See, I wrote these word but it was him I heard
Telling me how to set my spirit free
I'm not a poet I said, I just like to write
He rebuked that proclamation and set me down to type
And all my passion flowed from the deep
When I finished I cast my eyes upon the sea
Created from depths of me

I was shocked, I was afraid but still I continued to sit
Yes I stayed
I let the creator use me
And through this processes I have
And will have
To face many test
But each one I survive, he said
Moves me closer to my very best

This is how it was explained
And it took me a minute
For this to settle in my brain
I am my parents' daughter
My sisters- sister, someday maybe a mother
Someday maybe a wife
But without these relationships, these titles
Still, I have a greater good to serve
With this gift…my gift
He named life

Faith

I sought the world
Found faith
And the world sought me

Whispers

When the birds sing hear them say
"Your dreams are on their way."
When the wind blows listen to it call
"Your dreams are on their way."
Let water rush across your feet
At the shore line of the beach
Let the tied roll in then roll away
And listen to it say...
"Your dreams are on the way"
Rain drops dance across rooftops
It's calling out to you
In it's whisper you're hear it clearer
Your dreams are on their way

Don't let fear hold you back
Nor keep you down
Nor distract you from the bigger picture
Hear only the gentle whispers
That promises only the best
Let no man nor circumstance
Turn your truth into a test
Let the sun be the size of your faith
And fear will soon dissolve
Let hope be the moon
So that doubt will no longer call
Let the whispers sound like shouts
And carry you forward into every dream
Life is unfolding
And it's a beautiful thing
The shadows in the dark
May test your heart
But the whispers are protection
A reassurance of it all

I'm So Blessed!

I'm so blessed…
I wonder how anybody else can feel happy
I feel everything in this world is mine—all mine

Sometimes when I fancy foot, freely down the street
I have to stop myself from dancing
Because goodness is all under me, shaking the mess out of
Misery

Man, I am so blessed, that sometimes
And mind you, only some times I fill guilty
Because I know the secret of life
And even when others try to tell me their truth
So that I can receive it as my truth
I smile and like water, I flow out to sea.
My sea, where I see the realities of the world, my world

Man, I'm so blessed
That even when I don't have money things still get paid
When I've been in the worst way
A state of hands down, trump tight, full house, royally
flushed out luck, that man made experience, I'm blessed.
Blessed so strong that all I have to do is speak the words
Call into the Universe "HELP!"
All the world opens up and plenty goodness
Overtakes everything and anything out to do me in
Is removed

See I'm so Blessed
I don't have any problems
Now I have plenty assignments
And of course, they come with challenges great and small
But I'm so blessed that every challenge is just a game
To keep me playing with he puzzle until I get it right

I'm so blessed I don't know shortage
I only know Plenty
And she's always over extending herself to me
Now some times Plenty can get stingy
And act up just 'cause she can
But It's just her way of keeping me around
A little longer then I intended to stay
I'm so blessed I don't make mistakes
I mean, really
I never make, not a single mistake
Every thing I do, I do just right
Right up to the knowledge of my understanding
Of how far I am capable of excelling with the subject mater
At hand

Why I'm so blessed
That I know the meaning of
"Things don't just happen they happen just.
The way they are supposed to happen."
So I keep my eyes wide
My ears open, my arms up
And my palms giving thanks
Because…

I'm so blessed
I'm so Blessed I scare people
They so busy doing smack downs to their blessings
That they just want to mess with mine
But I know divinity and infinite bliss
So I hug them with my kindness
And love them with tenderness
And caress them with self-assurance
And they get scared of me
But even Fear is my friend
We go way back
I admit it. I do
In my youth I ran with Fear

Even had a long drawn out love affair with his buddy
Doubt
And let me tell you
Back in those days
Those brothers wore me out
Always making my nerves trimmer
And my head spin
Wow!
It seems silly to send my mind back
Warding off those days
But I was in it.
Young and naive
Thinking Doubt was what it was all about
And Fear just got power over me
But now I'm so Blessed
That those Brotha's won't even call me
You know, just to say "hello"
I guess they found some body like me
Back when
They were in
That's cool because every lesson I learned
Help me to this end
This end of being so Blessed
I'm so blessed I don't even cry no more
Every time I want to
I hear this voice saying
"What for?"
That didn't occur to make me sad or feel bad
No. The natural order of things must occur
Stopping it would be like cutting off the cord of life
I wouldn't want the world to stop spinning
Or night to never turn to day
Or winter to never be spring
So why cry over the Natural order of things?
I'm so blessed
I know how to make love
To 20 people at one time

While standing up
Fully clothed
Void of intermingling flesh
In silence
And in an empty room

I just hold steady my inner spirit
And channel together all the love and support they need
And I create
One love
Beyond any literal understanding

I have that much power
Because…
I'm so Blessed!

A Note from, Tyla, the Author...

Thank you for supporting
Red Wine and the Bles'sed Monkey
I welcome any comments or feedback. It has been a
wonderful journey. My greatest hope is that you have
enjoyed the journey with me. I welcome the opportunity
to participate in readings, book club meeting, events
and discussion. Feel free to contact me at
TYLA@IAMTYLA.COM

Meet and greet Tyla!

For the author's schedule and availability for
appearances at open mics, schools, churches
universities, mentoring programs, book fairs,
book clubs, literary events, expos and other
special events please e-mail:

Tyla

at

Tyla@IAMTYLA.com

www.IAMTYLA.com

Ordering Information

Red Wine and the Bles'sed Monkey

ISBN: 0-9722795-6-3

A Book By

Tyla

Red Wine and the Bles'sed Monkey is an intensely personal collection of poetry that invites its reader on a wonderfully complex journey into the heart and soul of a woman. She travels down the sometimes-abysmal path of life into the blissful realization of spiritual enlightenment. This powerful and thought-provoking collection speaks to the heart—embraces all in hopes of raising sensitivity to a universal level of compassion.

www.Amazon.com
Distribution: Baker & Taylor
Borders Books Nationwide
Specialty and Bookstores Nationwide
If not in stock, ask the store manager to:
Order via ISBN: 0-9722795-6-3
Retail Price: $14.95
Volume Discounts Available
http://www.EbonyEnergy.com
www.EbonyEnergyPublishing.com
www.GEMLiteraryFoundation.org
EbonyEnergy Publishing, Inc. (NFP)
A division of The GEM Group
P.O Box 43476
Chicago, IL 60643-0476
773-445-4946

EbonyEnergy Publishing

Passionately Printing One-Voice-At-A-Time

Real Voices by Real people

Eleven-Year-Old, Eric I. Keyes, III

The Light in the Dark

ISBN: 0-9722795-5-5

- **What was your biggest childhood fear? Were you afraid of monsters?**
- **Were you afraid of ghosts? I'll bet you were afraid of the dark!**

Eleven-year-old **Eric I. Keyes**, III helps children overcome their fears through his new book *The Light in the Dark*. Little Iggy learns that when he finds the courage to turn off his nightlight, there will be something amazing on the other side.

The first in an amusing series that celebrates encouragement, imagination, positive thinking, and self-discovery, *The Light in the Dark* encourages the fun of reading through rhythm, rhyme, and repetition. A complete educational resource, it features a glossary, journal, and book report page.

Don't delay. Order your copy of *The Light in the Dark* today!

The GEM Literary Foundation
A division of EbonyEnergy Publishing
P.O. Box 43476 Chicago, IL 60643-0476
773-851-5159 Mobile   773-445-4946 Office/Fax
1-818-992-5263 Media Agent/Availability
1-877-Kid -1-Book (1-877-543-1266) Orders
www.gemliteraryfoundation.org
E:Mail: books@gemliteraryfoundation.org
Retail Price: $14.99 Discounts Available/Full-Color/Paperback/Children: All Ages
40 Pages/ISBN: 0-9722795-5-5/Distribution: Baker & Taylor/Borders Book

About the Author

TYLA
ABERCRUMBIE

Tyla is a Chicago native who currently resides
in Los Angeles, California. A graduate of
Columbia College in Chicago, IL with a BA in Theatre
Tyla is an accomplished actor, writer, director, and spoken-
word performance artist. She is the Author of *Asylum (aka)
life, Psychological Terrorism and Naked and Raw,*
an one-act play told through poetry and music.